Nature's Children

CRABS

Jen Green

GROLIER
EDUCATIONAL

FACTS IN BRIEF

Classification of Crabs

Class: *Crustacea* (crustaceans)

Order: *Decapoda* (crabs, shrimps, and lobsters)

Suborder: *Brachyura* (true crabs)

Family: There are 47 families of true crabs.

Species: There are about 4,500 species of true crabs.

World distribution. Oceans and seashores worldwide.

Habitat. Sandy or rocky seashores and river estuaries. Some species live in deep water, while others live in warm, moist habitats on land.

Distinctive physical characteristics. Wide, flat body protected by a hard shell; 10 jointed legs; front pair of legs are developed into claws; small eyes on stalks; two pairs of antennae.

Habits. Crabs forage for scraps of food on seashores and in shallow water. Many species shelter in burrows or under rocks and are mainly active at night. Crabs reproduce by laying eggs.

Diet. Varied, includes shrimps, mussels, small animals, and plants.

© 1999 Brown Partworks Limited
Printed and bound in U.S.A.
Editor: James Kinchen
Designer: Tim Brown

Published by:

GROLIER
EDUCATIONAL

Sherman Turnpike, Danbury, Connecticut 06816

Library of Congress Cataloging-in-Publishing Data

Crabs.
p. cm. -- (Nature's children. Set 6)
ISBN 0-7172-9355-6 (alk. paper) -- ISBN 0-7172-9351-3 (set)
1. Crabs--Juvenile Literature. [1. Crabs.] I. Grolier Educational (Firm) II. Series.

QL444.M33G74 1999
595.3'86—dc21

98-33404

Contents

Strolling by the ocean on a lazy summer's day, you may be lucky enough to see a crab. Crabs are wary creatures and will probably scuttle for cover when they see you coming. Don't get too close! With their tough outer coats and nippy claws, these animals are easily able to defend themselves.

Crabs belong to a family of creatures called crustaceans. All the family members are protected by a hard, outer shell called a carapace. Distant relatives of crabs include woodlice and even barnacles, while lobsters, shrimps, and prawns are all close cousins. Most of these armored creatures live in water.

Crabs are the survival experts of the seashore. They know the ways of the oceans and live their lives in tune with the crashing waves. Crabs are amazing creatures and have some unusual friends and foes. Read on to find out more about them.

A crab is perfectly suited to life among the ocean waves.

Crab Country

Did you know that seas and oceans cover three-quarters of our planet? Most types of crabs live along the edges of the oceans, where the water meets the land. They spend part of their lives in salty seawater and part in air. Like fish, they have gills that can filter life-giving oxygen from the water. However, many crabs can also breathe air, allowing them to survive on land as well.

Crabs can be found in most of the watery habitats on Earth. Some crawl along the seabed, thousands of feet below the surface. Others inhabit freshwater streams and ponds. A few crabs spend most of their lives far from the ocean. They live in warm, moist places such as tropical rain forests.

These deep-sea crabs make their home in the warm water near an underwater volcano.

Although smaller than the giant spider crab, the spiny spider crab is still an impressive sight as it strides across the seabed.

Meet the Crab Family

How many types of crabs have you seen? You might have spotted a shore crab or a hermit crab on a trip to the seashore, or a blue crab, caught for food. There are about 4,500 different kinds of crabs, and they come in all different colors, shapes, and sizes.

The smallest members of the crab family are the pea crabs. These tiny critters are smaller than a pea even when full-grown! The largest crabs are the giant spider crabs that live off the coast of Japan. Their bodies are more than one foot (30 centimeters) across, and the distance between the tips of their outstretched claws may be as much as 10 feet (three meters)—the length of a small boat! You wouldn't want to meet one of these long-legged creatures on the beach!

Flat and Wide

Prawns and lobsters, close relatives of the crabs, have slender bodies ending in a long tail section called the abdomen. Crabs, on the other hand, are squat creatures, with wide, flat bodies. The head and middle parts of a crab's body are fused into a strong, armored box. Crabs have small tails that they keep tucked up underneath their bodies. Most types have short legs, but spider crabs have long, spindly legs, like a spider.

All crabs have 10 legs. The front pair of legs form the large, powerful claws that the crab uses to catch prey and defend itself. The other eight legs are smaller. They are used for scrambling about and swimming. Some crabs are expert swimmers. Their back legs are flattened like paddles and can be used to push strongly against the water.

A crab's flat body is perfect for squeezing into narrow crevices, out of the reach of predators.

Face to Face

Crabs have many senses that help them to find food and stay out of the way of enemies. All crabs have two pairs of feelers, or antennae, on their heads. The long pair help the crab to feel its way around the dark, cramped crevices of its rocky home. The short antennae allow the crab to smell and taste the water. The smell of a tasty morsel, such as a dead fish, wafting around the rockpool will soon have all the local crabs honing in for an easy meal.

Would you believe that a crab has three different sets of jaws? They all help to chomp and crush the crab's food into tiny pieces that are easy to digest.

Crabs have small, brightly colored eyes that look quite fierce and help keep enemies at bay. The eyes are found on the end of little stalks. Normally they stick out from the head, so the crab can see in all directions. If danger threatens, however, they can be pulled back inside the shell.

Opposite page:
If you were the same size as a crab, you wouldn't want to come face to face with one!

Legs Galore

Have you even done a fiddly task and wished you had an extra pair of hands? Or skidded on slippery ground and wished you had an extra pair of legs to steady you? Imagine if you had five pairs of legs, like a crab! A crab's legs are divided into thin, tubelike segments. The segments meet at bendy joints, like your knee joints. Each leg has several joints that bend at different angles, so the crab can move its legs in almost any direction.

Crabs have an amazing skill that helps them to overcome the dangers of the seashore. If a leg is injured, the crab can grow another one! The damaged limb breaks off at a special point near the body, where it causes hardly any bleeding. A new leg begins to grow at once, replacing the one that was lost.

This tiny spider crab's long legs help it to move easily over the coral reef on which it lives.

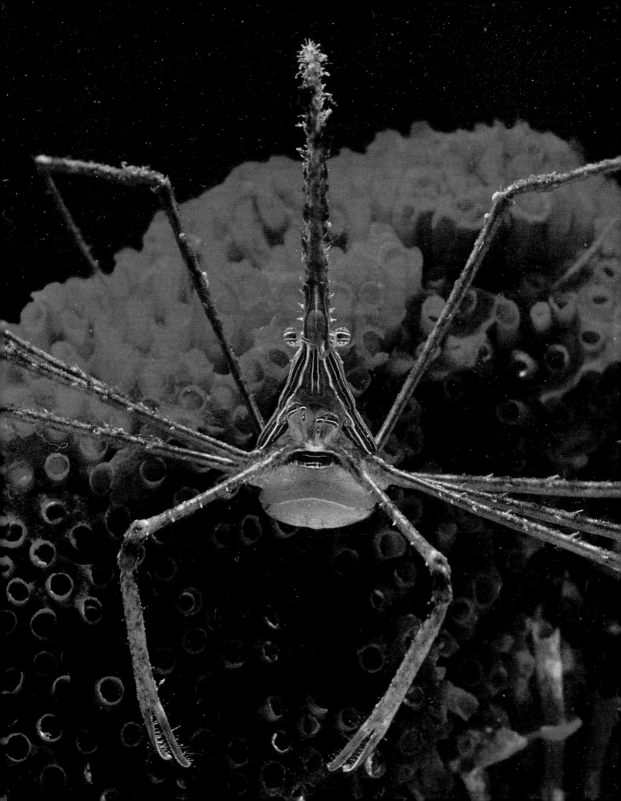

Clever Claws

A crab's prize possessions are its powerful front claws. With one fixed and one movable pincer, the claws can give you a nasty nip if you come too close! Claws are used for many different jobs. They can be waved menacingly to frighten enemies or used like tweezers to pick up a delicate morsel of food.

Crab claws come in many shapes and sizes, which help different kinds of crabs deal with their favorite foods. Some crabs have blunt, heavy claws that are great for crushing clam shells. Other crabs have slender claws that are just right for grasping slippery fish. Many crab's claws have sharp, toothed edges that make sure the crab's meal does not get away!

These red land crabs are using their strong legs and claws to cling to a slippery cliff.

A Suit of Armor

Hundreds of years ago knights rode into battle wearing suits of armor. The metal suits protected the knights' bodies against the blows of swords and spears. The armor was made up of many sections, so the knight could move his arms and legs. It kept him safe but was heavy, uncomfortable, and probably clanked whenever he moved!

A crab has a built-in suit of armor. Its hard shell protects the soft, delicate body parts inside. A crab's shell is also its skeleton, supporting its body from the outside. The shell is made of a tough material called chitin. Chalk from the crab's food and from seawater strengthens the shell and gives it extra weight.

Protected by its suit of armor, a porcelain crab shelters among the stinging tentacles of a sea anemone.

A Tight Squeeze

A crab's shell is a wonderful defense. Like the knight's suit of armor, however, it has its disadvantages, too. While it can be heavy and awkward, the biggest drawback is that there is no space inside for the crab to grow.

As a crab gets bigger, its armor gets tighter and tighter. The solution is to molt, or shed, the outgrown shell and start again. Grown-up crabs molt their shells once a year. As molting time approaches, the crab grows a new, soft skin underneath its shell. Then it swallows sea water, and its body swells up until its old armor splits down the middle. The crab scrambles backward out of its old shell and hides until its new skin hardens enough to protect it against its enemies.

On the Move

If you have ever seen crabs scuttling along a beach, you will know that they prefer to move sideways. With 10 legs and a wide, flat body, it quicker and easier for a crab to scuttle sideways than to move backward or forward. This way, it avoids tripping over its own legs.

In the crab world big does not generally mean fast. The largest crabs, Japanese spider crabs, move slowly on their long, spindly legs. On tropical seashores smaller ghost crabs race along at a much faster pace.

Long, sensitive hairs called setae on a crab's legs help the creature to feel its way over sand and pebbles. Sharp claws at the end of every leg keep a firm grip on slippery rocks and seaweed.

Defense Tactics

The seashore is a dangerous place for a small crab. At any moment a gull may swoop down, seize it by the leg, lift it high in the air, and dash it against the rocks. Animals that view crabs as a tasty treat include gulls, wading birds, and raccoons. Underwater enemies include fish, squids, and octopuses.

Crabs have a few tricks up their sleeves that help them to escape from enemies. When threatened, a crab may crouch down, tucking its legs beneath its armor-plated body. Alternatively, it may rear up with its claws held high, so it looks big and scary. Crabs are also good at hiding. They can bury themselves quickly in sand or scuttle under boulders.

Some crabs have surprise weapons that they use to defend themselves. In tropical waters boxer crabs hold a sea anemone in each claw. Enemies fear the anemone's stings and back off.

A wolf fish tries to make a meal out of a spider crab.

Vanishing Trick

For a crab the best way to keep safe is not to be seen at all. With shells that are shaped and colored to blend in with the natural world, crabs can be very hard to spot. This form of natural disguise, called camouflage, is used by many different types of animals.

Some crabs are camouflaged to look like shiny pebbles. Coral crabs resemble bits of broken coral. Velvet crabs have fine hairs on their backs that feel like velvet. The hairs trap grains of sand, so these crabs blend in with the sandy seabed. When ghost crabs stand quite still on a sandy seashore, you will never spot them against the background of the beach.

Resting on the colorful skin of a sea cucumber, this cucumber crab is perfectly camouflaged.

Disappearing in a cloud of sand, a blue crab digs itself out of trouble.

Masters of Disguise

Many crabs are camouflage experts. They go to a lot of trouble to make a disguise that will fool even the most sharp-eyed of hunters. Some spider crabs have long, thin legs that look like fronds of seaweed. They clip off pieces of real seaweed with their pincers and plant them on their backs to complete their disguise. If the seaweed dies, they replace it with a freshly clipped frond! Other crabs walk around with living sponges on their backs, pretending to be a sponge!

When danger threatens the masked crab, it quickly buries itself in the sand and hides with only its long antennae showing. Fine hairs on the antennae link together like the teeth in a zip to form a breathing tube. Using this built-in snorkel, the crab breathes oxygen-filled water and hides out under the sand until its enemy moves on.

No Place Like Home

For most crabs home is a little burrow dug into a rocky or sandy seashore. The muddy banks of a river estuary, washed by the salty tides, are also prime real estate for crabs. Using its legs and claws, a crab can dig itself a new burrow in just a few hours.

A few kinds of crabs have more unusual homes. The tiny pea crab lives inside the shell of a living oyster. In tropical rain forests the pine crab makes its home inside a plant called a bromeliad, which grows on the trunks of jungle trees. The leaves of the bromeliad join at its base to make a cup, where rainwater collects. The pine crab lives in this tiny pool, perched high among the tangled leaves and branches of the rain forest.

The mangrove tree crab lives among the leaves of mangrove trees that grow in tropical swamps.

The Hermit's Home

Crabs that live in burrows can never stray far from their homes. The hermit crab, however, gets around this problem by carrying its home on its back. Wherever the crab goes, its home goes too, like a tiny caravan.

The shape of hermit crabs' bodies are different from those of other crabs. Instead of a short tail section tucked under the body, the hermit has a long, fleshy tail without a shell. Lacking the natural armor of other crabs, the hermit seeks the shelter of an empty sea shell.

The hermit crab's back legs and tail are shaped to fit inside the shell and grip it tightly. When danger threatens, the crab pulls its body right inside its shell and uses a large, armored claw to block the entrance. Presented with this solid defense, the enemy usually gives up.

A hermit crab uses its strong front legs to haul its mobile home along the shore.

Moving House

From time to time, like other crabs, hermit crabs grow too big for their shells. When the hermit's shell becomes too tight, it must move home. Young hermit crabs often live in periwinkle shells and must switch to larger whelk shells as they grow.

The new, larger shell is checked out very carefully before the new owner moves in. First, the shell is tapped with a claw and rolled over to make sure that no one already lives there! The hermit then measures the new shell with its pincers, trying it out for size. When the crab is happy that all is well, it quickly lets go of its old shell and climbs into the new one tail-first. In seconds it is safe and sound inside its new, roomy home.

The hermit crab on the left is ready to move house, but this large shell is already occupied!

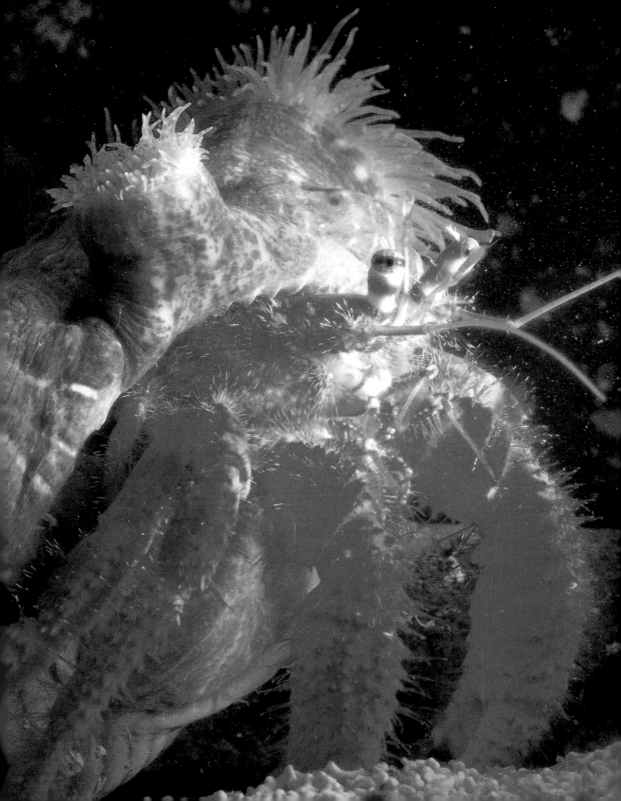

The Best of Friends

A hermit crab often shares its shell with several other creatures. A sea worm may live inside the shell. The worm eats scraps of the crab's food and helps to keep the crab's home nice and clean.

Besides the worm a sea anemone is often found clinging to a hermit crab's shell. The anemone also shares the crab's food. In return it helps to disguise the shell, and its stinging tentacles protect the crab from enemies.

The crab, the worm, and the anemone make a good team. They all help one another. In the natural world this type of friendship is called symbiosis. The crab likes living with the anemone and the worm so much that it will not leave them behind when it moves house. As soon as it is safe inside a larger shell, it picks them up in its pincers and carefully moves them to its new home.

The more the merrier! This hermit crab has several sea anemones clinging to its shell.

Feeding Time

Are you a picky eater, or do you eat anything that's going? Crabs are not fussy feeders. Their favorite foods are shrimps and mussels, but they will eat just about anything that comes their way. Crabs are scavengers, feeding on the remains of dead and dying animals. They are nature's cleaners and help to keep the seashore trim and tidy.

Some crabs have unusual eating habits. On tropical islands robber crabs feed on coconuts. These crabs are so large that their claws reach right around the trunk of a palm tree. The robber crab climbs the tree trunk and clips off a young coconut with its pincers. It drills into the coconut with its claws and feeds on the tasty flesh inside.

A robber crab feeds on a coconut. Robber crabs are closely related to hermit crabs and often live in snail shells before they reach full size.

The Rhythm of the Sea

Most crabs spend their lives by the ocean, within sight of the crashing waves. Their lives are ruled by the rhythm of the tides. When the tide is out, they hide in rockpools or bury down into the sand, where keen-eyed predators will not spot them. When the water returns at high tide, they come out of their holes to see what the sea has brought them. They sift through the sand and mud to find small creatures stranded by the waves.

Crabs seem to have a built-in clock that follows the sea's rhythm. They rest and feed in time with the tides, even if they are moved far from the sea. Most crabs are also nocturnal—they hide and rest by day and come out to look for food at night. By living like this, crabs avoid being out and about in daylight, when seabirds and other hunting animals are most likely to spot them.

Unlike most crabs, pink ghost crabs feed during the day, relying on their speed to protect them from hunters.

Take Your Partners

Like other animals, male and female crabs come together to mate and have young. In mangrove swamps male fiddler crabs go to a lot of trouble to attract a mate. To impress the females, each male stakes out his own territory—a small patch of the muddy shore that he defends against his rivals. Each male has one claw that is much bigger than the other, while the females have two small claws. He scuttles up and down his patch, shaking his large claw at other males to scare them away. Only the liveliest males with the biggest claws have any chance of attracting a mate. Unfortunately, the male's large claw is far too clumsy for collecting food, so males have to work twice as hard as females to get a meal!

A male fiddler crab has one small claw, which it uses to collect food, and one large claw for fighting rival males and attracting a mate.

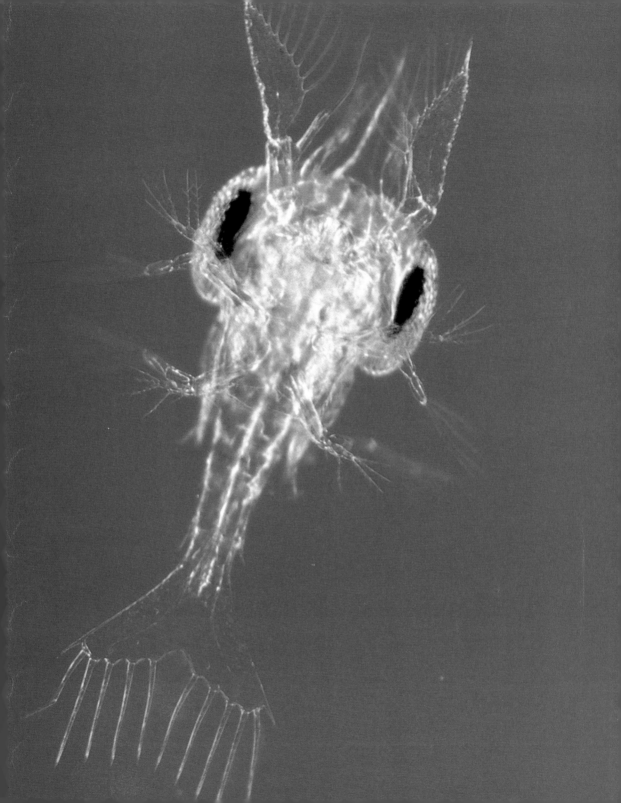

Crab Babies

How many children are there in your family?
Human parents have only a few children in
their lifetimes. They look after them very
carefully until they are grown up.

In the crab world things work differently.
Crab moms give birth to millions of babies,
but take no care of them at all. Most of the
young crabs die, but because there are so
many babies, a few will always survive.

Like most sea creatures, crabs reproduce by
laying eggs. Some female crabs simply release
their eggs into the water. Others keep their
eggs safe under their bodies, held in place by
their tails. A female hermit crab holds her eggs
inside her shell. After about three months the
eggs are fully developed, and the young crabs
hatch out and swim off into the ocean.

*A baby hermit crab does not look
much like its parents.*

Growing Up

A baby crab is a strange-looking critter. With a long tail, round body, and large eyes, it looks more like a tiny lobster than its mom or dad.

The young crab is called a larva. Unlike adult crabs, which live on the seabed, the larva swims at the surface of the ocean. It joins the plankton—a mixture of millions of tiny creatures that floats and drifts with the ocean currents. There is plenty to eat in the plankton, and the larva grows quickly. As it grows, it molts, or sheds, its skin many times. With every molt it looks a little more like its parents. After about five weeks the larva has turned into a tiny crab. At last it is ready to take its place on the seabed and learn the ways of its watery world.

Words to Know

Abdomen   The rear section of a crab's body.

Antennae   Feelers on a crab's head that are used for smelling, touching, and tasting.

Camouflage   Colors or patterns on an animal's body that help it to blend in with its surroundings and hide from predators.

Carapace   The hard, outer shell of a crab, lobster, or shrimp.

Gill   Part of an animal's body used for breathing underwater.

Larva   Young crab.

Molting   Shedding an old skin to make way for a larger one.

Predator   An animal that hunts and eats other animals for food.

Prey   An animal that is hunted and eaten by a predator.

Scavenger   An animal that eats dead or dying creatures.

Setae   Sensitive hairs that help a crab to feel and taste.

Symbiosis   A partnership between two different kinds of animals that helps both creatures to survive.

Territory   Area where an animal hunts or breeds, which it defends against other animals.

INDEX

Cover Photo: Peter Johnson / © Corbis
Photo Credits: Peter Johnson / © Corbis, pages 4, 22; Ralph White / Corbis, page 7; Michael Leach / NHPA, page 8; Lawson Wood / Corbis, pages 11, 24; Gerard Lacz / NHPA, page 12; Robert Pickett / Corbis, page 15; A.N.T. Photo Library / NHPA, pages 16, 39; Robert Yin / Corbis, pages 19, 27; Lynda Richardson / Corbis, page 28; Kevin Schafer / Corbis, page 31; Stuart Westmorland / Corbis, page 32; Trevor McDonald / NHPA, page 35; Daniel Heuclin / NHPA, page 36; Anthony Bannister / NHPA, page 40; Brandon D. Cole / Corbis, page 43; Image Quest 3-D / NHPA, page 44.